Page

Written and compiled by Mary Joslin
Illustrations copyright © 2009 Amanda Hall
This edition copyright © 2009 Lion Hudson

The moral rights of the author and illustrator
have been asserted

A Lion Children's Book
an imprint of
Lion Hudson plc
Wilkinson House, Jordan Hill Road,
Oxford OX2 8DR, England
www.lionhudson.com
UK ISBN 978 0 7459 4942 0
US ISBN 978 0 8254 7948 9

First edition 2009
This printing July 2009
10 9 8 7 6 5 4 3 2 1 0

Acknowledgments
Every effort has been made to trace and contact copyright
owners for material used in this book. We apologize for any
inadvertent omissions or errors.

All unattributed prayers are by Mary Joslin and Lois Rock,
copyright © Lion Hudson.
Prayers by Victoria Tebbs, Christina Goodings, Martin Paul and
Rebecca Winter are copyright © Lion Hudson.

"A Prayer for Songbirds" (p.48) by Joyce Denham is © Joyce
Denham, used by permission.
"We give thanks for domestic animals" (p.53) by Michael Leunig
is © Michael Leunig.
"Thank you, God, for sunshine" (p.59) by Mary Batchelor is
© Mary Batchelor, used by permission.
Prayer by Mother Teresa (p.93) used by permission.
Carmina Gadelica collected by Alexander Carmichael is published
by Floris Books, Edinburgh.

Bible extracts are taken or adapted from the *Good News Bible*,
the *Holy Bible, New International Version*, the *New Revised Standard
Version* and the *Authorized Version of the Bible (The King James Bible)*.
The *Good News Bible* is published by The Bible Societies/
HarperCollins Publishers Ltd, copyright © American Bible
Society 1966, 1971, 1976, 1992, used by permission.
The *Holy Bible, New International Version* is copyright © 1973,
1978, 1984 International Bible Society. Used by permission
of Zondervan and Hodder & Stoughton Limited. All rights
reserved. The 'NIV' and 'New International Version' trademarks
are registered in the United States Patent and Trademark Office
by International Bible Society. Use of either trademark requires
the permission of International Bible Society. UK trademark
number 1448790.
The *New Revised Standard Version* is published by HarperCollins
Publishers, copyright © 1989 by the Division of Christian
Education of the National Council of the Churches of Christ
in the USA, used by permission. All rights reserved.
Extracts from the *Authorized Version of the Bible (The King
James Bible)*, the rights in which are vested in the Crown, are
reproduced by permission of the Crown's Patentee, Cambridge
University Press.
The Lord's Prayer (on page 116) from *Common Worship: Services and
Prayers for the Church of England* (Church House Publishing, 2000) is
copyright © The English Language Liturgical Consultation, 1988
and is reproduced by permission of the publishers.

A catalogue record for this book is available
from the British Library

Typeset in 13/20 Latin 725 BT
Printed and bound in China by Printplus Ltd

Distributed by:
UK: Marston Book Services Ltd, PO Box 269, Abingdon,
Oxon OX14 4YN
USA: Trafalgar Square Publishing, 814 N Franklin Street,
Chicago, IL 60610
USA Christian Market: Kregel Publications, PO Box 2607,
Grand Rapids, MI 49501

THE LION BOOK OF
DAY-BY-DAY
PRAYERS

Written and compiled by MARY JOSLIN
Illustrated by AMANDA HALL

LION
CHILDREN'S

Contents

God help my thoughts! They stray from me, setting off on the wildest journeys; when I am at prayer, they run off like naughty children, making trouble. When I read the Bible, they fly to a distant place, filled with excitements. My thoughts can cross an ocean with a single leap; they can fly from earth to heaven, and back again, in a single second. They come to me for a fleeting moment, and then away they flee. Nothing can hold them back; no threats of punishment can restrain them. They slip from my grasp like tails of eels, they swoop hither and thither like swallows in flight.

Dear God, who can see into every heart, and read every mind, take hold of my thoughts. Bring my thoughts back to me, and clasp me to yourself.

Author unknown, adapted

Morning has broken

Quietly, in the morning,
I rise and look at the sky
To watch the darkness scatter
As sunlight opens the sky.
The day lies clear before me,
All fresh and shining and new,
And then I ask God to guide me
In all that I have to do.

*How clearly
the sky reveals
God's glory!
How plainly it
shows what he
has done!*

Psalm 19:1

Dawn

If you have heard
the sound of birdsong
in the morning air,
then you will know
that heaven's music
reaches everywhere.

Come into my soul, Lord,
as the dawn breaks into the sky;
let your sun rise in my heart
at the coming of the day.

Traditional

*May I glimpse
heaven in the
pure golden
sunrise.*

I am listening in the stillness
for the quiet whispers of creation
that tell me where God is moving
in the clear blue morning.

I will not hurry through this day!
Lord, I will listen by the way,
To humming bees and singing birds,
To speaking trees and friendly words;
And for the moments in between
Seek glimpses of thy great Unseen.

I will not hurry through this day;
I will take time to think and pray;
I will look up into the sky,
Where fleecy clouds and swallows fly:
And somewhere in the day, may be
I will catch whispers, Lord, from thee!

Ralph Spaulding Cushman

*This is the
day the Lord
has made;
let us rejoice
and be glad
in it.*

Psalm 118:24

Giving thanks

For this new morning and its light,
For rest and shelter of the night,
For health and food, for love and friends,
For every gift your goodness sends,
We thank you, gracious Lord.

Anonymous

Thank you, God in heaven
For a day begun.
Thank you for the breezes,
Thank you for the sun.
For this time of gladness,
For our work and play,
Thank you, God in heaven,
For another day.

Traditional

*May I treat
each new day
as a gift from
the giver of life.*

God has wrapped this day like a surprise present,
in the soft white mist of morning.

But look: an angel is untying the ribbons of
golden sunlight!

And there it is: a perfect, clear blue day for me.

*Learn from
the ants, you
lazybones.
They store up
their food
during the
summer for
the hungry
months of
winter.*

From
Proverbs 6:6–8

Rising

I rise from my bed
and turn away from idleness.

I wash in clear water
and resolve to keep my hands clean of wrongdoing.

I choose fresh clothes
and make myself ready for whatever tasks are mine.

I put on my shoes
and set my feet on the path of goodness and kindness.

I wake
I wash
I dress
I say:
"Thank you
God
for this
new day."

God, who hast folded back the mantle of the night
to clothe us in the golden glory of the day,
chase from our hearts all gloomy thoughts
and make us glad with the brightness of hope.

Ancient collect

*Start each day
with a fresh
beginning;
as if this
whole world
was made
anew.*

Motto from an
Amish school in
Pennsylvania

*I will keep
my solemn
promise to
obey God's just
instructions.*

From
Psalm 119:106

Morning resolutions

Do not follow the advice of the wicked,
but obey every word of God.

For the wicked are nothing more than wisps of straw in the
autumn gale; but the righteous are like trees that grow by
the lifegiving river, bearing leaves and fruit in their season.

From Psalm 1

O God,
There is so much to do today.
Help me to deal with each task, one by one.

O God,
May there be nothing in this day's work of which we shall be ashamed when the sun has set, nor in the eventide of our life when our task is done and we go to our long home to meet you face to face. Amen.

Walter Rauschenbusch (1861–1918)

Dear God,
Help me to
brighten this
day with
kindliness and
cheerfulness.

15

*Hold me,
dear God, and
I will be safe,
and I will
always pay
attention to your
commands.*

From
Psalm 119:117

For courage and kindliness

O God,
I will pray to you in the morning,
I will pray to you at sunrise.

I will ask you to show me the way that I should go.

I will ask you to protect me from the people who
do not like me, who want to hurt me.

I will trust in you to protect me,
I will trust in your love.

From Psalm 5

O God,
Help me to do what is good and right.
Save me from the longing to be popular and praised.
Save me from the fear of being mocked or ignored.
Help me to do what is good and right.

Hold on to what you believe in
Even if it is a tree which stands by itself.

Choose the path you believe to be right
Even if no others walk that way.

Trust in the power of everlasting love
Even if you feel you are all alone.

❖

Dear God,
Please keep me
upright and on
the right path.

17

*To you,
O Lord, I offer
my prayer;
In you, my God,
I trust.*

Psalm 25:1–2

I go forth today
in the might of heaven,
in the brightness of the sun,
in the whiteness of snow,
in the splendour of fire,
in the speed of lightning,
in the swiftness of wind,
in the firmness of rock.
I go forth today
in the hand of God.

Irish prayer (8th century)

Bless this house

Create a place of simplicity
In the quietness of your heart
With a window that looks to
    heaven
And a joy that will never depart.

19

Not one sparrow is forgotten by God... and you are worth much more than many sparrows.

From
Luke 12:6–7

Me

I am only me, but I'm still someone.
I cannot do everything, but I can do something.
Just because I cannot do everything does not give
    me the right to do nothing.

Motto from an Amish school
in Pennsylvania

Thank you for the year gone by
and all that I have done.
Thank you for my birthday
and the year that is to come.

Each and every day
this prayer, dear Lord, I pray:
make me wise to see
whom I should truly be.

God, who made the earth,
The air, the sky, the sea,
Who gave the light its birth,
Careth for me.

God, who made the grass,
The flower, the fruit, the tree,
The day and night to pass,
Careth for me.

God, who made all things,
On earth, in air, in sea,
Who changing seasons brings,
Careth for me.

Sarah Betts Rhodes (1824–1904)

*Dear God,
make me brave
enough to choose
a life of joy.*

*May I value
truth, wisdom,
learning and
good sense.*

From
Proverbs 23:23

My everyday life

Oh, you gotta get a glory
In the work you do;
A Hallelujah chorus
In the heart of you.

Paint, or tell a story,
Sing, or shovel coal,
But you gotta get a glory,
Or the job lacks soul.

Anonymous

May my hands be helping hands
For all that must be done
That fetch and carry, lift and hold
And make the hard jobs fun.

May my hands be clever hands
In all I make and do
With sand and dough and clay and things
With paper, paint and glue.

May my hands be gentle hands
And may I never dare
To poke and prod and hurt and harm
But touch with love and care.

*May I
remember
today the
lessons I learned
yesterday.*

23

*Homes are
built on the
foundation of
wisdom and
understanding.
Where there
is knowledge,
the rooms
are furnished
with valuable,
beautiful
things.*

Proverbs 24:3–4

Our home

Bless the window
Bless the door
Bless the ceiling
Bless the floor
Bless this place which is our home
Bless us as we go and come.

24

Bless the mess
but make us strong
to put our things
where they belong.

God bless the house from roof to ground,
With love encircle it around.
God bless each window, bless each door,
Be Thou our home for evermore.

Dear God, bless those who visit us: family, friends
and strangers. May we make our home a place of
love and kindness for all. May we share the things
we have with generosity and cheerfulness.

Victoria Tebbs

*A house
shelters the
body; but
love shelters
the soul.*

Make your father and mother proud of you; give your mother that happiness.

Proverbs 23:25

My family

Dear God, bless all my family,
as I tell you each name;
and please bless each one differently
for no one's quite the same.

Dear God,
Help me to hear the wise things my mother says.
Help me to hear the wise things my father says.

In all the times we've loved and laughed
And fought and rowed and hated
We give a cautious thanks for those
To whom we are related.

I give thanks for the people
who are my home:
we share a place to shelter;
we share our food;
we share our times of work
and play and rest;
we share our lives.

Help parents to understand their children.
Help children to understand their parents.

From Ephesians 6:1–4

*May every
family give its
members the
support they
need to stand
alone.*

*O God,
What a rich
harvest your
goodness
provides!*

From
Psalm 65:11

Around the table

All good gifts around us,
Are sent from heaven above,
Then thank the Lord, O thank the Lord,
For all his love.

Matthias Claudius (1740–1815), translated by
Jane Montgomery Campbell (1817–78)

Let us take a moment
To thank God for our food,
For friends around the table
And everything that's good.

Bless this food
And those who made it;
Bless this food
And we who ate it.

Seed, earth, sun, rain,
Root, leaf, fruit, grain,
Pick, wash, chop, heat,
Give thanks: now eat.

The harvests have ripened in the sun;
There's plenty of food for everyone:
There's some for ourselves and more to share
With all the world's people everywhere.

The bread is warm and fresh,
The water cool and clear.
Lord of all life, be with us,
Lord of all life, be near.

African grace

*F*or health
and strength
and daily food,
we praise your
name,
O Lord.

Traditional

29

*You may
make your plans,
but God directs
your actions.*

Proverbs 16:9

With God you must let things begin,
With God let all things come to rest;
In this way the work of your hands
Will flourish and also be blessed.

Translated from David Beiler's
Bible bookplate, 1845

Worldwide family

We share the earth
we share the sky
we share the shining sea
with those we trust
with those we fear:
we are God's family.

*Dear friends,
let us love one
another, because
love comes
from God.*

1 John 4:7

The circle of friendship

O God,
We give thanks for the goodhearted people who
love us and do good to us and who show their
mercy and kindness by providing us with food and
drink, house and shelter when we are in trouble or
in need.

From a 1739 prayer book

Dear God,
May we who are friends look inwards to support
  one another
And outwards to welcome others as new friends.

May friendship last
even when we are forgetful.

May friendship last
even when we are busy.

May friendship last
even when we are tired.

May friendship last.

Dear God,

May we sit down with friends through all our days:

On the plastic chairs of playgroup,

On the wooden chairs at school,

On the soft and sagging sofas of home,

On the folding chairs of holidays,

On the fashionable seats of restaurants

And on the dusty seats in the garden

Till at last, when we have grown old,

We need our friends to help us in and out of chairs.

*Dear God,
Help me to be
a friend to
someone who
needs a friend.*

My community

May our town be a safe place:
by day and by night,
for young and for old,
for rich and for poor,
for people of every colour and every faith.
May we be a community.

Dear God,
When I see someone in trouble,
may I know when to stop and help
and when to hurry to fetch help;
but may I never pass by,
pretending I did not see.

Based on Jesus' parable of
the Good Samaritan, Luke 10:25–37

*May everyone
in our
community
feel at home
in it.*

Dear God,

We pray for minorities: for the little groups of people whose
needs are overlooked; the people whose voices are not heard;
the people who do not have much power.

Help us to find ways to help them in our community.
Help us to find ways to make the government notice them.
Help us to work for justice in our own country.

Dear God,

Be very close to people who have been hurt by crime.
Help them in their shock and helplessness
and shower them with kindness and love.

35

*J*esus said,
*"Love your
enemies."*

From
Matthew 5:44

Those we fear

O God,
Close my ears to the whispering and the sniggering and the
name-calling of those who want to torment me.

Close my ears to ignore them, and open my mouth to tell on
them: not because I am mean, but because I am brave enough
to stop their nastiness spreading even further.

O God,
You created us to enjoy your goodness.
You created me,
you created those I love,
and you created those who hate me
to enjoy your goodness together.

We pray for the people who are condemned as wicked:
those who are responsible for wars and massacres
and terrorism.

We pray that people of good faith will find a way
to stop them.

We also pray that you and we will treat them with
justice and mercy.

Dear God,
I am not ready to forgive
but I am ready to be made ready.

We will find our safety
not within encircling walls
but within a circle of friendship.

*There is more
to a human
being than
the worst thing
they ever did.*

*When you give
to the poor, it is
like lending to
the Lord, and
the Lord will
pay you back.*

Proverbs 19:17

A better world

There's trouble in the fields, Lord,
The crops are parched and dry.
We water them with tears, Lord,
So help us, hear our cry.

There's trouble in our hearts, Lord,
The world is full of pain.
Set us to work for healing,
Send blessings down like rain.

Lord, watch over refugees,
their tired feet aching.
Help them bear their heavy loads,
their bent backs breaking.
May they find a place of rest,
no fears awake them.
May you always be their guide,
never forsake them.

Give strength, dear God, to the brave people who
   go to help places that are torn apart by disasters.
Keep them safe.
Help them to know what is the right thing to do.
Turn their efforts into miracles.

O God,
We are all strangers in this world
and we are all travelling to your country.

So may we not treat anyone as a foreigner or an outsider,
but simply as a fellow human being
made in your image.

*Dear God,
Please accept
our tiny
offerings
and do great
things with
them.*

*O God,
Settle disputes
among the
nations, among
the great powers
near and far.*

From Micah 4:3

Peace at last

Dear God,
Take care of those who live in war zones:

Afraid of noise,
afraid of silence;

Afraid for themselves,
afraid for others;

Afraid to stay,
afraid to go;

Afraid of living,
afraid of dying.

Give them peace in their hearts,
in their homes
and in their land.

Blessed are the peacemakers, for they will
be called children of God.

From Matthew 5:9

Where the bombs are falling
let there be only rain.

Where the bullets are whistling
let there be only wind.

Where wars have left the land bleak and bare
let there be a springtime of peace.

*Dear God,
Give us the
courage to
overcome anger
with love.*

*Try to be at
peace with
everyone, and
try to live a
holy life.*

Hebrews 12:14

O God,
Gather together as one
those who believe in peace.
Gather together as one
those who believe in justice.
Gather together as one
those who believe in love.

All things bright and beautiful

All things bright and beautiful,
All creatures great and small,
All things wise and wonderful,
The Lord God made them all.

Cecil Frances Alexander (1818–95)

ALL THINGS
BRIGHT AND
BEAUTIFUL

❖

*O Lord,
Your greatness
is seen in all
the world!*

Psalm 8:9

Wonderful world

Here on the ancient rock of earth
I sit and watch the sky;
I feel the breeze that moves the trees
While stately clouds float by.
I wonder why our planet home
Spins round and round the sun
And what will last for ever
When earth's days all are done.

White are the wavetops,
White is the snow:
Great is the One
Who made all things below.

Green are the grasslands,
Green is the tree:
Great is the One
Who has made you and me.

Blue are the cornflowers,
Blue is the sky:
Great is the One
Who made all things on high.

Gold is the harvest,
Gold is the sun:
God is our Maker –
Great is the One.

ALL THINGS
BRIGHT AND
BEAUTIFUL

❖

*Who can
question God,
who laid the
cornerstone of
the world?*

From Job 38:6

ALL THINGS
BRIGHT AND
BEAUTIFUL

❖

*God is the king
of even the king
of beasts.*

Based on
Job 41:34

All God's creatures

I think of the diverse majesty
Of all of the creatures on earth;
Some with the power to terrify
Others that only bring mirth.
I think of their shapes and their colours,
Their secret and curious ways,
And my heart seems to long for a language
To sing their Great Maker's praise.

Praise God for the animals:
For the colours of them,
For the spots and stripes of them,
For their claws and paws.

Lynn Warren

When God's kingdom comes
the wolves and sheep will live together in peace,
and leopards will lie down with young goats.
Calves and lion cubs will feed together
sharing the same pasture.

Little children will take care of them
and snakes will not inflict any poison.
There will be nothing harmful or evil
and the whole world will honour God.

From Isaiah 11

ALL THINGS
BRIGHT AND
BEAUTIFUL

❖

O God,
*May we give
your creatures
the respect they
deserve.*

47

Songbirds

The God of gods protect you
In wind, and hail, and storm;
In summer, keep you cool;
In winter, keep you warm.

The God of gods supply you
With water and with seed,
With perch and branch and house,
And safety as you feed.

The God of gods be watching,
Lest one of you should fall;
Attending every move;
And hearing every call.

The God of gods uplift you,
and speed you in your flight;
Direct you to a sheltered roost,
And keep you snug at night.

The God of gods inspire you,
And fill your heart with song;
Trill greetings in the morning,
And praises all day long.

Joyce Denham, "A Prayer for Songbirds"

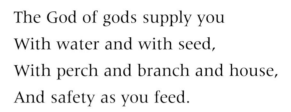

When I see the birds go soaring,
wheeling, dipping through the sky,
Deep inside my spirit longs
to learn to fly.

The wild birds are calling out
their wild morning song
to praise the Maker God
to whom wild things belong.

❖

*"My little
sisters the birds,
you ought to
sing God's
praise at all
times and in
all places."*

Saint Francis
of Assisi
(1181–1226)

Green and growing

The trees grow down,
down into the earth,
right down into long ago.

The trees grow up,
up into the sky,
right up where the strong winds blow.

The trees, they sway,
they sway in the wind
and whisper a secret song:

"We thank you, God,
for keeping us safe,
that we might grow tall and strong."

O God,
You show your care for the land by sending rain;
you make it rich and fertile.
You fill the streams with water;
you provide the earth with crops.

Wherever you go there is plenty.
The whole world sings for joy.

From Psalm 65

*May we,
like leaves,
reach out to
light and life.*

I open my hands
to God's golden sunshine.
I fold my hands
in God's silver light.
I reach up tall
to touch God's blue heaven.
I trust in God
to grow up aright.

Creator God
fashion designer to the flowers
is bringing out
this season's collection.

ALL THINGS
BRIGHT AND
BEAUTIFUL

❖

*May we learn
from the ant
the season for
hard work.*

From
Proverbs 6:6–8

The little things

The little bugs that scurry,
The little beasts that creep
Among the grasses and the weeds
And where the leaves are deep:
All of them were made by God
As part of God's design.
Remember that the world is theirs,
Not only yours and mine.

He prayeth best, who loveth best
All things both great and small;
For the dear God who loveth us,
He made and loveth all.

Samuel Taylor Coleridge (1772–1834)

I think the butterfly
says her prayer
by simply fluttering
in the air.

I think the prayer
of the butterfly
just dances up
to God on high.

We give thanks for domestic animals.
Those creatures who can trust us enough to come
close. Those creatures who can trust us enough to
be true to themselves.

They approach us from the wild. They approach us
from the inner world. They bring beauty and joy,
comfort and peace.

For this miracle and for the lesson of this miracle,
we give thanks.

Amen.

Michael Leunig

ALL THINGS
BRIGHT AND
BEAUTIFUL

❖

*Thank you,
Maker God, for
the creatures
that cheer and
comfort us.*

*The world and
all that is in it
belong to the
Lord.*

Psalm 24:1

Our God is the God of all,

The God of heaven and earth,

Of the sea and the rivers;

The God of the sun and of the moon
and of all the stars;

The God of the lofty mountains and
of the lowly valleys,

He has His dwelling around heaven and
earth and sea, and all that in them is.

St Patrick (389–461)

Pattern of seasons

I will remember the buds of spring
When summertime leaves are green;

I will remember their rippling shade
When colours of autumn of seen;

I will remember the red and the gold
When wintertime branches are bare;

I will give thanks to the God of the trees
Whose love reaches everywhere.

*For everything
there is a season,
and a time for
every matter
under heaven.*

Ecclesiastes 3:1

Around the year

O Year, grow slowly. Exquisite, holy,
The days go on.
With almonds showing, the pink stars blowing,
And birds in the dawn.

Grow slowly, year, like a child that is dear,
Or a lamb that is mild,
By little steps, and by little skips,
Like a lamb or a child.

Katharine Tynan
(1861–1931)

God bless the birds of springtime
that twitter in the trees
and flutter in the hedgerows
and soar upon the breeze.

God bless the birds of summer
that gather on the shore
and glide above the ocean
where breakers crash and roar.

God bless the birds of autumn
as they prepare to fly
and fill the damp and chilly air
with wild and haunting cry.

God bless the birds of winter
that hop across the snow
and peck the fallen seeds and fruits
of summer long ago.

*Through the
circling years
we climb the
spiral stairway
to heaven.*

PATTERN OF
SEASONS

❖

*God sets
the time for
planting.*

From
Ecclesiastes 3:2

Spring

God has lit each wintry bough
with tiny flames of green,
and soon the woods will be ablaze
as springtime leaves are seen.

All is well:
the leaves of grass are growing.
All is well:
the leaves of flowers are showing.
All is well:
the leaves of trees are blowing.
All is well:
God's springtime love is showing.

Thank you, God, for sunshine,
Thank you, God, for spring,
Thank you, God, for sending
Every lovely thing.

Mary Batchelor

Merrily, merrily,
All the spring,
Merrily, merrily
Small birds sing.
All through April,
All through May,
Small birds merrily
Carol all day.

Rodney Bennett

*Give thanks
for the world's
awakening.*

*It is good to
be able to enjoy
the pleasant
light of day.*

Ecclesiastes 11:7

Summer

Let me drift like a seagull
up in the summer sky
feeling the air grow golden
as the sun rises high.

Let me drift like a seagull
out on the sea so wide
feeling the ocean moving
as the moon pulls the tide.

Let me drift through the summer
down by the ocean shore
resting in God's creation
now and for evermore.

The waves roll in from the glittering green
of the sparkling summertime sea.
They curl and unfurl on the golden sand
and run up the beach to me.

The waves roll out to the beautiful blue
where the ocean touches the sky.
They swish and they slide with the silver tide
and shyly they say goodbye.

Thank you, God, for this summer day;
Thank you, God, for this golden day;
Thank you, God, for this lazy day;
Thank you, God, for this holiday.

*Take delight
in the
golden days
of summer.*

*God sets
the time for
harvesting.*

From
Ecclesiastes 3:2

Autumn

Thank you, dear God, for our harvest garden.
Thank you for the seeds and the soil,
for the sun and the rain,
for the roots and the leaves and the ripening fruits.
As you have blessed us with harvest gifts, dear God,
may we bless others by sharing them.

Autumn berries
round and red:
by God's hand
the birds are fed.

*Give thanks
for the
abundance of
the earth.*

The Lord is good to me,
And so I thank the Lord
For giving me the things I need,
The sun, the rain, the appleseed.
The Lord is good to me.

Attributed to John Chapman, American
pioneer and planter of orchards
(1774–1845)

The gold leaves now turn to rust,
the silver clouds to grey;
we give thanks for the autumn
as the summer slips away.

*At God's
command…
storm winds
come from
the south, and
biting cold from
the north.*

From Job 37:5, 9

Winter

Now the wind is coming,
Now the wind is strong,
Now the winter freezes
And the darkness will be long.
Now we see the starlight
In the midnight sky,
We know God is with us
And the angels are close by.

O thought I!
What a beautiful thing
God has made winter to be
by stripping the trees
and letting us see
their shapes and forms.
What a freedom does it seem
to give to the storms.

Dorothy Wordsworth (1771–1855)

*The bare trees
of winter let us
see the heavens
more clearly.*

I stand to gaze at the pure white snow
new from heaven on earth below.

Dear God,
Thank you for the wild tangle of the
    woodlands
and the murky damp of ditch and bog.
Thank you for the sharp smell of crumble
    and decay
and for the winter wet in which old things
    pass away.

*Have reverence
for God, and
obey his
commands,
because this
is all that
human beings
were created for.*

Ecclesiastes 12:13

Some prayers seem to belong in spring meadows:
full of hope.

Some prayers seem to belong by the summer ocean:
full of joy.

Some prayers seem to belong to the autumn forest:
full of wisdom.

Some prayers seem to belong to the winter wasteland:
full of pain.

All these prayers belong to God:
God of the changing years.

A fragile world

Our little woodland planet
basks in the light of the vast universe
like a wild flower
on a rocky mountainside.

We must cherish it.

*Do you not
know? Were
you not told long
ago? Have you
not heard how
the world began?*

Isaiah 40:21

God's world

Most high, most great and good Lord, to you belong praises, glory and every blessing; to you alone to they belong, most high God.

May you be blessed, my Lord, for the gift of all your creatures and especially for our brother sun, by whom the day is enlightened. He is radiant and bright, of great splendour, bearing witness to you, O my God.

May you be blessed, my Lord, for our sister the moon and the stars; you have created them in the heavens, fair and clear.

May you be blessed, my Lord, for our brother the wind,
for the air, for cloud and calm, for every kind of weather,
for through them you sustain all creatures.

May you be blessed, my Lord, for our sister water, which is
very useful, humble, pure and precious.

May you be blessed, my Lord, for our brother fire, bright,
noble and beautiful, untamable and strong, by whom you
illumine the night.

May you be blessed, my Lord, for our mother the earth,
who sustains and nourishes us, who brings forth all kinds
of fruit, herbs and brightly coloured flowers.

Saint Francis of Assisi (1182–1226), "Canticle of the Sun"

*It was made
by the one who
sits on his throne
above the earth
and beyond the
sky.*

Isaiah 40:22

*God stretched
out the heavens
and laid
the earth's
foundations.*

From Isaiah 51:13

A world consumed

We think the earth is ours.

We dig it, drill it, plough it, mine it, pave it, bomb it.

Then, from within the heart of things, the earth erupts:
it shakes, it quakes, it shifts, it drifts.

May we learn to respect the earth, for it is shaped by forces
greater than our own, and we should live in awe of them.

Dear God,
May we not grow too proud of our buildings:
our tall towers
our deep tunnels
our long bridges.

May we remember that they are laid upon the foundations
of the earth,
the earth that belongs to you.

We give thanks for streetlamps that shine on our path,
but oh! for a glimpse of the stars
that wheel their way through the heavens above
with Jupiter, Venus and Mars.

We give thanks for pavements without ruts or holes,
but oh! for the smell of the earth,
the feel of tussocks and tree-roots and mud,
the planet that gave us our birth.

*It is not walls
that make a
city strong,
but justice and
righteousness.*

*The mountains
and hills may
crumble, but
God's love will
never end.*

From Isaiah 54:10

Making amends

Our world is fallen
as if from heaven.

Our world is broken
so we shall mend it.

Our world is wounded
so we shall heal it.

Our world is the Lord's
and God will bless it.

The winter brook flows quick and green
with swirling eddies in between
its tiny falls of sparkling spray
that curl and ripple on their way.

The summer brook is slow and grey
and choked with all we've thrown away:
old cans and bags and battered shoes
and things that we no longer use.

Dear God, our Maker, send the rain
to wash the whole world clean again
then teach us to respect and care
for fire, water, earth and air.

God's world is full of litter
and what we plan to do
is go and pick it up to make
the whole world good as new.

*Dear God,
Forgive for the
ways we have
squandered
the earth.*

*God can turn
the desert into
pools of water
and dry land
into flowing
springs.*

From Isaiah 41:18

Growing green

Create a space for little things:
Bejewelled bugs with buzzing wings
And pudgy grubs that bravely cling
To slender stems that bend and swing.

Create a calm for quiet things:
For timid birds too shy to sing
And breaths of wind that softly linger
In the blossom trees of spring.

Christina Goodings

Bind the wounded earth, dear Lord,
in bandages of green
and heal the scars where storm and flood
and lightning fire have been.

I am a weed, I come to heal
The poor scarred earth, each wound and weal.
So silently I spread my root
Full well before I start to shoot.

I rise up from a muddy trench
Despite the rubbish, filth and stench
And then defend the woodland glades
With leaves as sharp as razor blades.

I raise my hordes of airborne seeds
And train them up for daring deeds
To implement the plot I've planned
To bind down every grain of sand,

To capture from the sun and rain
The power to fill the world again.
We are the weeds: we really mean
To wrap the whole wide world in green.

Martin Paul

❖

*D*ear God,
*Give life to
the seeds we sow
and the trees
we plant.*

*The desert will
rejoice, and
flowers will
bloom in the
wilderness.*

Isaiah 35:1

At peace with the planet

May the earth be kind to everyone:
pure cool water, flowing;
clean and clear air, blowing;
crops in good earth, growing;
golden sunshine, glowing.
May everyone be kind to the earth.

Let there be space for the flooding,
Let there be space for the storm,
Let there be space for the cosy place
Where we can be snug and warm.

*O God,
Remind us of
our duty to
cherish the
earth.*

Save me a clean stream, flowing
to unpolluted seas;

lend me the bare earth, growing
untamed flowers and trees.

May I share safe skies
when I wake, every day,

with birds and butterflies?
Grant me a space where I can play

with water, rocks, trees, and sand;
lend me forests, rivers, hills, and sea.

Keep me a place in this old land,
somewhere to grow, somewhere to be.

Jane Whittle

*God says this:
"I am making
a new earth and
new heavens…
Be glad and
rejoice for ever
in what
I create."*

Isaiah 65:17, 18

Lord of the ocean,
Lord of the sea:
Let all the fish swim
Strong and free.

Lord of the wavetops,
Lord of the shore:
Keep them all safe
For evermore.

Day-by-day prayers

Day by day,
dear Lord, of thee
three things I pray:
to see thee more clearly,
love thee more dearly,
follow thee more nearly,
day by day.

Richard, bishop of Chichester
(1197–1253)

*It is better to
have wise people
reprimand you
than to have
stupid people
sing your
praises.*

Ecclesiastes 7:5

Monday: Wisdom

Who may come into God's presence?

The person who obeys God in everything,
who always speaks the truth,
who keeps every promise,
who cannot be lured into doing wrong.

Such a person will be safe all through life.

From Psalm 15

Dear God,
Help me to grow up good.

Help me not to make mistakes just because
  I am young.

Help me to be righteous without being smug;
faithful to you without being narrow-minded;
loving without being naïve;
peaceable without being weak.

Help me, dear God, because I ask you.

Based on 2 Timothy 2:22

Dear God,
Help me to find the right way to go,
even though the gate to it be narrow,
and the path difficult to walk.

Based on Matthew 7:13

*May I live
today more
wisely than
yesterday so I
may be gladder
tomorrow.*

Hate what is evil, love what is right, and see that justice prevails.

Amos 5:15

Tuesday: Justice

When I have to choose
between right and wrong
help me make the right choice
and give me peace in my heart.

From Colossians 3:15

Lord Jesus,
Make me as kind to others
as I would want to be to you.

Make me as generous to others
as I would want to be to you.

May I take time to help them
as I would want to take time to help you.

May I take trouble to help them
as I would want to take trouble to help you.

May I look into the faces of those I meet
and see your face.

Based on Matthew 25:37–40

*Just and
merciful God,
help me to be
fair and
forgiving.*

Dear God,
Help me not to speak evil of anyone, but to be peaceful
and friendly, and always to show a gentle attitude
towards everyone.

From Titus 3:2

God says this:
If you put an end to oppression, to every gesture of
contempt, and to every evil word; if you give food to
the hungry and satisfy those who are in need, then the
darkness around you will turn to the brightness of noon.
And I will always guide you and satisfy you with good
things.

From Isaiah 58:9–11

Dear God,
Make me good
so I can be a
blessing
to others.

Based on
Proverbs 10:7

Wednesday: Self-control

May I be no one's enemy, and may I be the friend of that which lasts for ever.

May I never quarrel with those nearest: and if I do, may I be quick to restore the friendship.

May I love only what is good: always seek it and work to achieve it.

May I wish for everyone to find happiness and not envy anyone their good fortune.

May I never gloat when someone who has wronged me suffers ill fortune.

When I have done or said something wrong, may I not wait to be told off, but instead be angry with myself until I have put things right.

May I win no victory that harms either me or those who compete against me.

May I help those who have quarrelled to be friends with each other again.

*May I do
the things that
will still seem
right when
I look back
on them.*

May I, as far as I can, give practical help to my friends and anyone who is in need.

May I never fail a friend who is in danger.

When I visit those who are grieving, may I find the right words to help heal their pain.

May I respect myself.

May I always control my emotions.

May I train myself to be gentle and not allow myself to become angry.

May I never whisper about wicked people and the things they have done, but rather seek to spend my time with good people and to follow their good example.

Eusebius (3rd century, adapted)

*The road the
righteous travel
is like the
sunrise, getting
brighter and
brighter until
daylight has
come.*

Proverbs 4:18

Thursday: Endurance

There is no place where God is not,
wherever I go, there God is.
Now and always he upholds me with his power
and keeps me safe in his love.

Author unknown

In the face of evil and wrongdoing
I will surely not be happy,
Nor will I let myself grow too sad.
Instead, I will choose to stand up for what is right
And I will face the future
With calm and courage and cheerfulness.

Who would true valour see,
Let him come hither;
One here will constant be,
Come wind, come weather.
There's no discouragement
Shall make him once relent
His first avowed intent
To be a pilgrim.

Whoso beset him round
With dismal stories,
Do but themselves confound;
His strength the more is.
No lion can him fright,
He'll with a giant fight;
But he will have a right
To be a pilgrim.

Hobgoblin nor foul fiend
Can daunt his spirit;
He knows he at the end
Shall life inherit.
Then fancies fly away,
He'll fear not what men say;
He'll labour night and day
To be a pilgrim.

John Bunyan (1628–1688)

*Walk with me,
O God, however
long the journey.*

*I believe that I
will not have to
wait for heaven
to know God's
goodness.*

From Psalm 27

Friday: Faith

You are holy, Lord, the only God,
and your deeds are wonderful.

You are strong.
You are great.
You are the Most High,
You are almighty.
You, holy Father, are
King of heaven and earth.

You are Three and One,
Lord God, all good.
You are Good, all Good, supreme Good,
Lord God, living and true.

You are love,
You are wisdom.
You are humility,
You are endurance.
You are rest,
You are peace.
You are joy and gladness.
You are justice and moderation.
You are all our riches,
And you suffice for us.

*Faith is like
a tree, reaching
for heaven's
light through
the forest of
doubt.*

You are beauty.
You are gentleness.

You are our protector,
You are our guardian and defender.
You are courage.
You are our haven and our hope.

You are our faith,
Our great consolation.
You are our eternal life,
Great and wonderful Lord,
God almighty,
Merciful Saviour.

St Francis of Assisi (1181–1226)

*We have
placed our hope
in the living
God, who is the
Saviour of all.*

1 Timothy 4:10

Saturday: Hope

Help me to be patient as I wait for your kingdom
and your righteousness:
as patient as a farmer who trusts that the rains
will come in their season,
and that the land will produce its harvest.
Keep my hopes high.
Help me to pray to you and to praise you.

I wait eagerly for the Lord's help
and in his word I trust.
I wait for the Lord
more eagerly than watchmen wait for the dawn.

Psalm 130:5–6

O God,
be to me
like the evergreen tree
and shelter me in your shade,
and bless me again
like the warm gentle rain
that gives life to all you have made.

Based on Hosea 14:4–8

*O God,
Give me
new hope
with every
sunrise.*

I cast my prayer on the river
and let it float to the sea
and over the far horizon
and off to eternity.

*Whoever loves
is a child of
God and knows
God… for God
is love.*

From
1 John 4:7–8

Sunday: Love

O God,
Let me learn how to love.
May I grow more patient.
May I speak more kindly.
May I act more humbly.
May I never give up learning to love.

Based on 1 Corinthians 13

Teach me, O God,
to do what is just,
to show constant love
and to live in fellowship with you.

Based on Micah 6:8

Dear God,
Help me to love you with all my heart,
with all my soul and with all my mind.

Help me to love those around me as much as
I love myself.

Based on the words of Jesus from Matthew 22:34–40

Love is giving, not taking,
mending, not breaking,
trusting, believing,
never deceiving,
patiently bearing
and faithfully sharing
each joy, every sorrow,
today and tomorrow.

> Anonymous

O God,
as truly as you are our father,
so just as truly you are our mother.
We thank you, God our father,
for your strength and goodness.
We thank you, God our mother,
for the closeness of your caring.
O God, we thank you for the great love
you have for each one of us.

> Julian of Norwich (1342–after 1416)

*We can do
no great things,
only small
things with
great love.*

Mother Teresa
of Calcutta
(1910–97)

*Love the Lord
your God and
serve him with
all your heart.*

Deuteronomy
11:13

To faith, let me add goodness;
to goodness, let me add knowledge;
to knowledge, let me add self-control;
to self-control, let me add endurance;
to endurance, let me add godliness;
to godliness, let me add affection for my
   brothers and sisters;
to affection, let me add love.

From 2 Peter 1:5–7

The Christian year

Harvest time is gold and red:
Thank you, God, for daily bread.
Christmas time is red and green:
Heaven now on earth is seen.
Easter time is green and white:
Bring us all to heaven's light.
Pentecost is white and gold:
God's own spirit makes us bold.

A child is born to us! A son is given to us! And he will be our ruler.

Isaiah 9:6

Advent and Christmas

Let us travel to Christmas
By the light of a star.
Let us go to the hillside
Right where the shepherds are.
Let us see shining angels
Singing from heaven above.
Let us see Mary cradling
God's holy child with love.

God, our loving Father, help us remember the birth of Jesus, that we may share in the song of the angels, the gladness of the shepherds and the wisdom of the wise men.

May the Christmas morning make us happy to be your children and the Christmas evening bring us to our beds with grateful thoughts, forgiving and forgiven, for Jesus' sake.

Amen

Robert Louis Stevenson (1850–94)

The stars that shine at Christmas
Shine on throughout the year;
Jesus, born so long ago,
Still gathers with us here.
We listen to his stories,
We learn to say his prayer,
We follow in his footsteps
And learn to love and share.

He will be called, "Wonderful Counsellor", "Mighty God", "Eternal Father", "Prince of Peace".

Isaiah 9:6

Look, your king is coming to you! He is humble and rides on a donkey.

From
Zechariah 9:9

Holy Week

Dear God,
May I welcome you as my king:
King of peace,
King of love,
King in death,
King of life.

There is a green hill far away,
Outside a city wall,
Where the dear Lord was crucified
Who died to save us all.

There was no other good enough
To pay the price of sin;
He only could unlock the gate
Of heaven, and let us in.

O, dearly, dearly has he loved,
And we must love him too,
And trust in his redeeming Blood,
And try his works to do.

Cecil Frances Alexander (1818–95)

Lord Jesus, who died upon the cross:
You know this world's suffering,
You know this world's sorrowing,
You know this world's dying.

In your name, Lord Jesus, who rose again:
I will work for this world's healing,
I will work for this world's rejoicing,
I will work for this world's living.

*He endured
the suffering
that should have
been ours…
because of our
sins he was
wounded.*

Isaiah 53:4, 5

Jesus, you are the light of the world.
May we live our lives as you taught, so that your light
will shine through us in all we think and say and do.

Dear God,
Help me to love other people so well that they
recognize me as one of your friends and loyal followers.

Based on John 13:34–35

*The angel
asked, "Why
are you looking
among the dead
for one who is
alive?"*

From
Luke 24:5

Easter

Good Friday is locked in winter,
in grief and death and dark;
Easter Sunday begins the springtime,
rising up like the lark.

The tree of thorns
is dressed in white
for resurrection day;
and joy springs from
the underworld
now death is put away.

We celebrate Easter with the disciples who saw the
    risen Jesus,
and who knew that love was stronger than death.

We also remember Thomas, for whom Easter was
    a long time coming,
and all those who feel alone in their doubt and despair
    this Easter.

Risen Jesus, make yourself known to us all in due time
so we may know for sure the joy of heaven.

*"He is not
here; he has
been raised."*

Luke 24:6

*T*hose who
are led by
God's Spirit
are God's
children.

Romans 8:14

Pentecost

Let God's Spirit come
like the winds that blow:
take away my doubts;
help my faith to grow.

Let God's Spirit come
like a flame of gold:
warm my soul within;
make me strong and bold.

May the words I speak
tell others of Jesus.

May the things I do
tell others of Jesus.

May my whole life
tell others of Jesus.

Based on James

Spirit of God
put love in my life.

Spirit of God
put joy in my life.

Spirit of God
put peace in my life.

Spirit of God
make me patient.

Spirit of God
make me kind.

Spirit of God
make me good.

Spirit of God
give me faithfulness.

Spirit of God
give me humility.

Spirit of God
give me self-control.

From Galatians 5:22–23

❖

*The Spirit
has given us
life; the Spirit
must also
control our
lives.*

Galatians 5:25

Live in such a way as to cause no trouble either to Jews or Gentiles or to the church of God.

1 Corinthians
10:32

Special days

Thank you, dear God, for all the good things with which
  you have blessed us.
Thank you for your love in good times; thank you for your
  unfailing love in difficult times.
Thank you for your promise to be with us always.
Amen.

A prayer of thanksgiving

Jesus' body,
Broken bread,
By God's word
We all are fed.

Jesus' lifeblood,
Wine that's spilt,
As one temple
We are built.

At this table
Take your place:
Feast upon
God's love and grace.

A prayer for holy
communion

Help me, Lord,
to be quiet and still,
to hear your voice
to know your will.

Help me, Lord,
to sing loud and clear,
to praise your name
through all the year.

A prayer for a church service

*May I imitate
those who
have set an
example of the
Christian life;
mostly, may
I imitate Christ.*

Based on
1 Corinthians 11:1

Dear God,
Thank you for the example of other Christians. From
the stories of their faith, may I grow in understanding.
From the stories of their kind-hearted deeds, may I
learn to do good.

A prayer for a saint's day

Pay attention to God's laws; do away with evil; keep the festivals.

From
2 Kings 22, 23

Go, and know that the Lord goes with you:
let God lead you each day
into the quiet place of your heart,
where he will speak with you;
know that he loves you and watches over you –
that he listens to you in gentle understanding,
that he is with you always,
wherever you are and however you may feel:
and the blessings of God – Father, Son
and Holy Spirit – be yours for ever.

Rebecca Winter

Praying with the Bible

Lord, hear my prayer!

Remind me each morning of your constant love,
for I put my trust in you.
My prayers go up to you;
show me the way I should go.

Psalm 143:1, 8

107

*Worship the
Lord with joy;
come before
him with
happy songs!*

Psalm 100:2

Praising God

Praise the Lord!

Praise the Lord from heaven,
you that live in the heights above.
Praise him, all his angels,
all his heavenly armies.

Praise him, sun and moon;
praise him, shining stars.
Praise him, highest heavens,
and the waters above the sky.

Let them all praise the name of the Lord!
He commanded, and they were created;
by his command they were fixed in their places for ever,
and they cannot disobey.

Praise the Lord from the earth,
sea monsters and all ocean depths;
lightning and hail, snow and clouds,
strong winds that obey his command.

Praise him, hills and mountains,
fruit trees and forests;
all animals, tame and wild,
reptiles and birds.

Praise him, kings and all peoples,
princes and all other rulers;
young women and young men,
old people and children too.

Let them all praise the name of the Lord!
His name is greater than all others;
his glory is above earth and heaven.
He made his nation strong,
so that all his people praise him –
the people of Israel, so dear to him.

Praise the Lord!

Psalm 148

*God made us,
and we belong
to God.*

Psalm 100:3

*Let us come
before God with
thanksgiving
and sing joyful
songs of praise.*

Psalm 95:2

Thanking God

The Lord is my shepherd;
I have everything I need.
He lets me rest in fields of green grass
and leads me to quiet pools of fresh water.
He gives me new strength.
He guides me in the right paths,
as he has promised.
Even if I go through the deepest darkness,
I will not be afraid, Lord,
for you are with me.
Your shepherd's rod and staff protect me.

You prepare a banquet for me,
where all my enemies can see me;
you welcome me as an honoured guest
and fill my cup to the brim.
I know that your goodness and love will be with me
   all my life;
and your house will be my home as long as I live.

Psalm 23

Give thanks to the Lord, because he is good;
his love is eternal.
Give thanks to the greatest of all gods;
his love is eternal.
Give thanks to the mightiest of all lords;
his love is eternal.

He alone performs great miracles;
his love is eternal.
By his wisdom he made the heavens;
his love is eternal;
he built the earth on the deep waters;
his love is eternal.

He made the sun and the moon;
his love is eternal;
the sun to rule over the day;
his love is eternal;
the moon and stars to rule over the night;
his love is eternal.

Give thanks to the God of heaven;
his love is eternal.

Psalm 136:1–9, 26

*The Lord has
done great
things for us,
and we are glad.*

From
Psalm 126:2, 3

*God, have
pity on me,
a sinner!*

Luke 18:13

Confession

Be merciful to me, O God,
because of your constant love.
Because of your great mercy
wipe away my sins!

I recognize my faults;
I am always conscious of my sins.
I have sinned against you – only against you –
and done what you consider evil.
So you are right in judging me.

Sincerity and truth are what you require;
fill my mind with your wisdom.

Create a pure heart in me, O God,
and put a new and loyal spirit in me.

Give me again the joy that comes from your salvation,
and make me willing to obey you.

From Psalm 51

I told God everything:
I told God about all the wrong things I had done.
I gave up trying to pretend.
I gave up trying to hide.
I knew that the only thing to do was to confess.

And God forgave me.

Based on Psalm 32:5

Come back to the Lord your God.
He is kind and full of mercy;
he is patient and keeps his promise;
he is always ready to forgive and not punish.

Joel 2:13

*If you forgive
others the
wrongs they
have done to
you, your
Father in
heaven will
also forgive
you.*

Matthew 6:14

113

*The laws of
the Lord are
right, and
those who
obey them are
happy.*

Psalm 19:8

Living wisely

O Lord,

How can young people keep their lives pure?

By obeying your commands.

With all my heart I try to serve you;

keep me from disobeying your

commandments.

From Psalm 119:9–10

O Lord,

I have heard your commandments.

May I worship you.

May I worship you alone.

May all I say and do show respect for your holy name.

May I honour the weekly day of rest.

May I show respect for my parents.

May I reject violence so that I never take a life.

May I learn to be loyal in friendship and so learn to be
faithful in marriage.

May I not steal what belongs to others.

May I not tell lies to destroy another person's reputation.

May I not be envious of what other have, but may I learn
to be content with the good things you give me.

Based on the Ten Commandments, Exodus 20

Jesus said,
"Now I give
you a new
commandment:
love one
another."

From John 13:34

*Ask, and
you will receive;
seek, and you
will find; knock,
and the door
will be opened
to you.*

Matthew 7:7

The prayer Jesus taught

Our Father in heaven:
May your holy name be honoured;
may your Kingdom come;
may your will be done on earth as it is in heaven.
Give us today the food we need.
Forgive us the wrongs we have done,
as we forgive the wrongs that others have done to us.
Do not bring us to hard testing,
but keep us safe from the Evil One.

Matthew 6:9–13

Our Father in heaven,
hallowed be your name,
your kingdom come,
your will be done,
on earth as in heaven.
Give us today our daily bread.
Forgive us our sins
as we forgive those who sin against us.
Lead us not into temptation
but deliver us from evil.

For the kingdom, the power,
and the glory are yours
now and for ever.
Amen.

The Lord's Prayer

Father:
May your holy name be honoured;
may your Kingdom come.
Give us day by day the food we need.
Forgive us our sins,
for we forgive everyone who does us wrong.
And do not bring us to hard testing.

Luke 11:2–4

*Your Father
in heaven will
give good things
to those who
ask him.*

From
Matthew 7:11

117

*To you alone,
O Lord, must
glory be given,
because of
your constant
love and
faithfulness.*

From Psalm 115:1

I love the Lord, because he hears me;
he listens to my prayers.
He listens to me every time I call to him.

The Lord is merciful and good;
our God is compassionate.

Be confident, my heart,
because the Lord has been good to me.

Psalm 116:1–2, 5, 7

Life's journey

I am a pilgrim
on a journey
to the place
where God is found;
every step
along that journey
is upon
God's holy ground.

*G*od says this:
"Do not cling
to events of the
past or dwell on
what happened
long ago."

Isaiah 43:18

Changes

Thank you, dear God,

for the blessing of things that stay the same:

for people we have known for ever

and the familiar paths where we walk.

Thank you, dear God,

for the blessing of things that change:

for newcomers with their new customs,

new ways of doing things, new paths to discover.

Thank you, dear God,

for the blessing of the old and the blessing of the new.

Dear God,

We have arrived at this, our new home, feeling

as lost as windblown seeds that are dropped

upon the earth.

Let us put down roots here where we have

landed, and let our lives unfold in your love

and light.

Father, lead us through this day
As we travel on our way.
Be our safety, be our friend,
Bring us to our journey's end.

A tiny boat
a great big sea
a guardian angel
watching me.

❖

"*Watch for
the new thing I
am going to do…
I will make a
road through the
wilderness.*"

Isaiah 43:19

*Do not imitate
what is bad,
but imitate
what is good.*

3 John 11

A new school

Dear God,

The holidays are over and a new school year begins. May it be for us all a new start: a chance to surprise ourselves with what we can achieve, a chance to astonish others with our previously hidden talents and a new opportunity for friendship and trust.

Goodbye, dear old school,
Hello, bright new start.
May God guide our lives,
Head and hand and heart.

Dear God,
It's so hard to go against the in-crowd and be kind to someone everybody hates. Give me courage and help me to imagine what that person must be feeling.

Victoria Tebbs

Dear God,
I resolve this
day to do what
is right,
even if no one
else will join me.

Dear God,
Help us as we learn new things. If we learn quickly and easily, may we help others to understand. If we make mistakes, may we understand what went wrong. Help us never to be afraid of new things, but to see them as an adventure.

❖

*Do your best
in the race, run
the full distance,
and keep the
faith.*

From
2 Timothy 4:7

Fresh challenges

This day is full of promises
of everything that's good;
help me face its challenges
and do the things I should.

Dear God,
Bless this practice time.
May I get better at doing things right,
Not faster at doing things wrong.

When new tasks feel like a wall,
help me find the door.

When new tasks feel like a mountain,
help me find the path.

When new tasks feel like the trackless desert,
help me find a guide.

*Take
fresh courage
every day.*

As I learn to swim,
keep my legs from sinking.

As I learn to swim,
keep my head from sinking.

As I learn to swim,
keep my heart from sinking.

As I learn to swim,
keep my spirits from sinking.

Teach us, Lord,
to serve you as you deserve,
to give and not to count the cost,
to fight and not to heed the wounds,
to toil and not to seek for rest,
to labour and not to ask for any reward
save that of knowing that we do your will.

St Ignatius Loyola (1491–1556)

O God,
Be good to me,
and guide me
on a safe path.

Psalm 143:10

Journeys

Walking alone,
just me and God;
alone, just God and me.

Walking along
and trusting God
knows where I want to be.

My journey may be fast or
My journey may be slow;
May God be always with me
Wherever I may go.

❖

May I travel bravely and return safely.

Dear God,

We have a complicated journey ahead.

We want all its parts to join up into one smooth journey.

We want to arrive safely, with all our belongings.

We ask you to make things go well for us,

and to give us courage to deal with any problems.

Alone with none but thee, my God,

I journey on my way.

What need I fear, when thou art near

O king of night and day?

More safe am I within thy hand

Than if a host did round me stand.

St Columba (521–97)

Lord, watch over me as I journey,

do not let me travel too far.

May I return in the light of this day

to the place where my friends and faith are.

❖

*T*rust in
the Lord and
do good.

Psalm 37:3

Farewells

We stand at a parting of the ways.
We thank God for the companionship we have enjoyed,
for the things we have done together
and the things we have learned together.

We ask God to bless us as we go our separate ways,
knowing that there will be uphills and downhills,
good times and bad times.

We pray that we will find new friendships and new
   challenges.
We pray that God will give us faith and hope at all times,
and surround us with unfailing love.

Walk the way of kindness,
Walk the way of right,
Walk the way of wisdom,
Walk the way of light.

May the white-winged angels
Encircle thee around.
May they guide thy footsteps
Upon the holy ground.

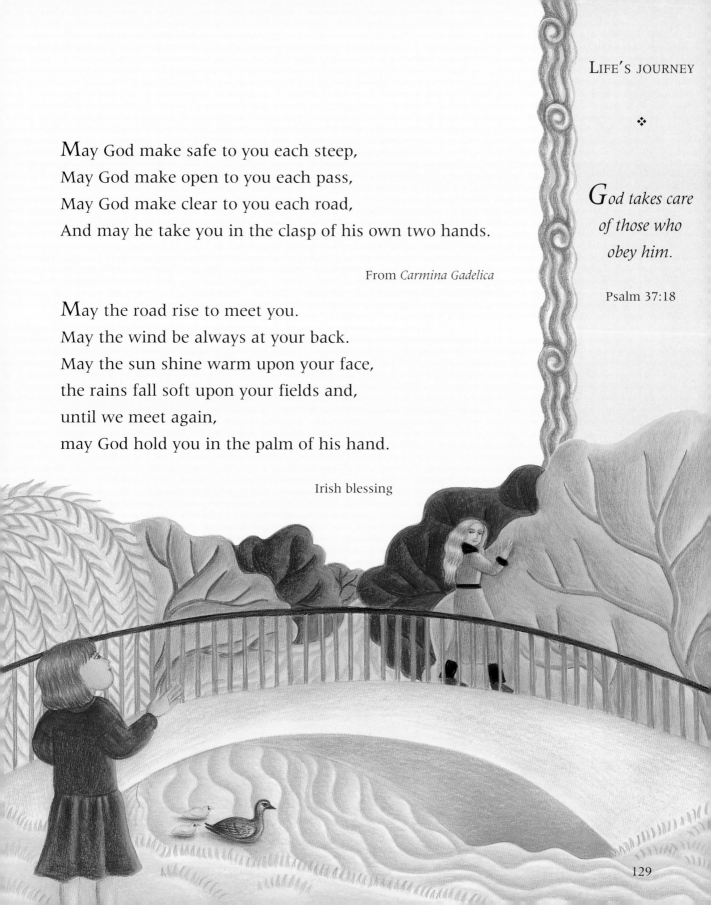

❖

God takes care of those who obey him.

Psalm 37:18

May God make safe to you each steep,
May God make open to you each pass,
May God make clear to you each road,
And may he take you in the clasp of his own two hands.

From *Carmina Gadelica*

May the road rise to meet you.
May the wind be always at your back.
May the sun shine warm upon your face,
the rains fall soft upon your fields and,
until we meet again,
may God hold you in the palm of his hand.

Irish blessing

❖

God's love and mercy never fail; they are new every morning, as sure as the sunrise.

From
Lamentations
3:22, 23

May the strength of God pilot us.

May the power of God preserve us.

May the wisdom of God instruct us.

May the hand of God protect us.

May the way of God direct us.

May the shield of God defend us.

May the host of God guard us against the snares
of evil and the temptations of the world.

St Patrick (389–461)

Sad times

God is our shelter and strength,
always ready to help in times of trouble.
So we will not be afraid, even if the earth is shaken
and mountains fall into the ocean depths;
even if the seas roar and rage,
and the hills are shaken by the violence.

Psalm 46:1–3

*God is good
to everyone who
trusts in him.*

Lamentations 3:25

Feeling sad

I have been crying in the night, O God;
my pillow is wet with tears.
I am too tired to face the day,
too scared to face those who hate me.

Keep me safe from those evil people;
listen to my cry for help.
Bring all their wickedness to an end;
answer my prayer.

From Psalm 6

Lord, make me an instrument of your peace.
Where there is hatred, let me sow love;
Where there is injury, pardon;
Where there is discord, union;
Where there is doubt, faith;
Where there is despair, hope;
Where there is darkness, light;
Where there is sadness, joy.

O divine Master, grant that I may not so much seek to be
consoled as to console, to be understood as to understand,
to be loved as to love; for it is in giving that we receive,
it is in pardoning that we are pardoned, and it is in dying
that we are born to eternal life.

Attributed to St Francis of Assisi (1181–1226)

*God's love
for us is sure
and strong.*

Lamentations 3:32

God knows when we are crushed, when we are treated unjustly.

From
Lamentations
3:34–36

Feeling worried

O God,
I am uncertain.
I am afraid.
My imagination runs wild.
Perhaps the earth will crumble beneath me
and I will fall into endless darkness.

O God,
Keep my feet on holy ground
and shine the golden light of heaven on my path.

The Lord is my light and my salvation;
I will fear no one.
The Lord protects me from all danger;
I will never be afraid.

Psalm 27:1

Keep watch, dear Lord, with those who work, or watch, or weep this night, and give your angels charge over those who sleep.

St Augustine (354–430)

I will not worry, dear God,
but I will ask you for the things I need
and give thanks.

Give me the peace that comes from knowing that all
my worries are safe with you.

From Philippians 4:6–7

*God loves you,
so don't let
anything worry
you or frighten
you.*

Daniel 10:19

Lord, I have given up my pride
and turned away from my arrogance.
I am not concerned with great matters
or with subjects too difficult for me.
Instead, I am content and at peace.
As a child lies quietly in its mother's arms,
so my heart is quiet within me.

Psalm 131:1–2

When you pass through deep waters, God will be with you.

A last goodbye

Dear God,
You lend us to this world
to love one another.

Now we must say goodbye
to someone we love
and who loved us.

At this time of parting,
may they know more of your love,
and may we know more of your love.

Amen.

As the rain hides the stars, as the autumn mist hides
the hills, as the clouds veil the blue of the sky, so the
dark happenings of my lot hide the shining of your face
from me. Yet, if I may hold your hand in the darkness,
it is enough. Since I know that, though I may stumble
in my going, you do not fall.

Gaelic prayer (translated by Alistair MacLean)

Dear God,
I am missing someone so badly.
There is a hole in my days,
in my evenings,
in my life.
Dear God,
How can I survive the pain
of missing?

O God,
Protect my heart
from the grief
of goodbye.

O God,
May we learn from the seasons
the beauty of living
and the grace of dying.

*God says this:
"I will never
forget you…
I have written
your name on
the palms of
my hands."*

From
Isaiah 49:15, 16

Remembering

Every day
in silence we remember

those whom we loved
to whom we have said a last goodbye.

Every day
in silence we remember.

We lay flowers
and remember this person.

We lay flowers
and remember the sad times.

We lay flowers
and remember the glad times.

We lay flowers
and remember God's love.

SAD TIMES

❖

O *God,*
Never forget the
one we loved.

We give them back to you dear Lord, who gavest them to us.
Yet as thou didst not lose them in giving,
so we have not lost them by their return.
For what is thine is ours always, if we are thine.

Quaker prayer

My candle burns; its tiny light
shines to make this dark place bright.

My candle burns, a flame of love
shining up to heaven above.

*Jesus said,
"I am the
resurrection
and the life."*

John 11:25

Thinking of heaven

I stand on the sand by the edge of the sea
and watch the waves roll by;
I look to the faraway misty line
where water touches sky;
I look at the shapes of the clouds in the blue
dissolving into space;
I dream of the heaven where God can be found,
where I will see God's face.

My life flows on in endless song;
Above earth's lamentation
I hear the sweet though far-off hymn
That hails a new creation:
Through all the tumult and the strife
I hear the music ringing;
It finds an echo in my soul –
How can I keep from singing?

What though my joys and comforts die?
The Lord my Saviour liveth;
What though the darkness gather round!
Songs in the night he giveth:
No storm can shake my inmost calm
While to that refuge clinging;
Since Christ is Lord of heaven and earth,
How can I keep from singing?

Robert Lowry (1826–99)

Let dark earth
be a place of rest;
let bright heaven
be a place of peace.

*Those who
believe in Jesus
will live, even
though they die.*

From
John 11:25

SAD TIMES

❖

*God is making
a new earth
and new
heavens.
Be glad and
rejoice.*

From
Isaiah 65:17, 18

Flood of sorrow, flood of tears
Like the flood of ancient years

Now in grief my world is drowned
Storm and cloud are all around

Pull me to the ark of love
Set your rainbow high above

Let my world grow new and green
Let the tree of peace be seen.

Safe this night

Day is done,
Gone the sun
From the lake,
From the hills,
From the sky.
Safely rest,
All is well!
God is nigh.

Anonymous

At close of day

The morning clouds are orange and pink
As the sun climbs into the sky,
And white clouds drift in the faraway blue
At noon when the sun is high.
The sunset mixes up purple and mauve
With violet, gold and red,
And angels watch over me through the dark
When I'm asleep in my bed.

Walk with me in golden sun
Walk with me in rain
Walk with me in happiness
Walk with me in pain.

Walk with me at morning time
When the world is light
Walk with me when evening comes
Watch me through the night.

Thank you, dear God, for the day just gone.
I wasn't happy all the way through:
there was a time when it seemed that all my plans were ruined.
Then, out of the very thing that went wrong,
came the best thing of all.
Now I know for sure
that you blessed me.

SAFE THIS
NIGHT

❖

*At the end
of the day,
we remember
God's blessings
with
thankfulness.*

145

SAFE THIS
NIGHT

❖

*God made the
moon and stars,
and set them in
their places.*

From
Psalm 8:3

Moon and stars

The moon is afloat on the heavenly sea
And I wait on dreamland's shore;
Dear God, let me sleep
Through the dark so deep
Until the night is no more.

The moon shines bright,
The stars give light
Before the break of day;
God bless you all
Both great and small
And send a joyful day.

Traditional

I stand in the presence of the infinite beauty of the stars.
I stand in the presence of the infinite beauty of the moon.
I stand in the presence of the infinite beauty of the sky.
I stand in the presence of the infinite.

The sunrise
tells of God's glory;
the moonrise
tells of God's glory;
the starshine
tells of God's glory;
the heavens
tell of God's glory.

Based on Psalm 19

*Open my eyes,
dear God, to
the beauty of
the night.*

*God will not
let you fall;
your protector
is always
awake.*

Psalm 121:3

In the dark hours

Father God,
I am awake in the night,
and all alone,
like so many others.
Some are afraid: give them courage.
Some are worried: give them hope.
Some are sad: give them comfort.
Some are just tired: give them sleep.

In the quiet night,
I can hear the wind
that blows from heaven,
bringing life and hope
to all the earth.

*When darkness
falls, dear God,
be our light.*

My room is dark
in deepest night:
O fill my life
with heaven's light.

I am awake
to unknown fear:
O send the angels
very near.

Then let me
softly fall asleep
till sunbeams
through the window creep.

O God,
I am awake in the night and afraid:
afraid because I cannot see clearly
but instead imagine all manner of things.

O God,
Turn my mind to pleasant imaginings
and turn my imaginings to happy dreams
and turn my happy dreams to quiet sleep again.

Safe this night

When I lie down, I go to sleep in peace; you alone, O Lord, keep me perfectly safe.

Psalm 4:8

Lord, keep us safe this night,
Secure from all our fears;
May angels guard us while we sleep,
Till morning light appears.

John Leland (1754–1841)

Send your peace into my heart, O Lord,
that I may be contented
with your mercies of this day and confident
of your protection for this night;
and having forgiven others,
even as you forgive me,
may I go to my rest in peaceful trust
through Jesus Christ, our Lord. Amen.

St Francis of Assisi (1181–1226)

Clouds in the sky above,
Waves on the sea,
Angels up in heaven
Watching over you and me.

Christina Goodings

Now I lay me down to sleep,
I pray thee, Lord, thy child to keep;
Thy love to guard me through the night
And wake me in the morning light.

Traditional

SAFE THIS
NIGHT

❖

*May my
waking hours
be innocent
and my dreams
untroubled.*

151

*May the
grace of the
Lord Jesus be
with everyone.*

Revelation 22:21

Blessings

May the Lord bless you and take care of you;

May the Lord be kind and gracious to you;

May the Lord look on you with favour and give you peace.

Numbers 6:24–26

Wherever you go,

May God the Father be with you.

Wherever you go,

May God the Son be with you.

Wherever you go,

May God the Spirit be with you.

Be thou a bright flame before me,

Be thou a guiding star above me,

Be thou a smooth path below me,

And be a kindly shepherd behind me,

Today, tonight, and for ever.

From *Carmina Gadelica*

Deep peace of the running waves to you,
Deep peace of the flowing air to you,
Deep peace of the quiet earth to you,
Deep peace of the shining stars to you,
Deep peace of the shades of night to you,
Moon and stars always giving light to you,
Deep peace of Christ, the Son of Peace, to you.

Traditional Gaelic blessing

*Jesus said,
"Peace is what
I leave with you;
it is my own
peace that I
give you."*

John 14:27

Index of first lines

M

N

O

W

Y